A Month of Sundays

the New Mexico columns

HARRY MUSSELWHITE

EDITED BY RICHARD JAY HUTTO

ISBN 978-7357604-6-9

cover and book design: Dekie Hicks
photography: Harry Musselwhite

Wheredepony Press
Rome, Georgia

To Henry

Splendid Harry! We met when he was co-running the Rome Film Festival and have been friends ever since. He won me over instantly, when Dorothy and I were down there for the festival, by singing "Yesterday" in his deep basso at a private gathering.

Harry is multi-talented—acts, sings, does voice-overs, writes—actually what can't he do? This is a man with a broad frame of reference! And these essays reflect that in the best way. He's acted for me, sung for me, supported my efforts, and now I'm happy to recommend this great series of pieces.

John Hancock,
Academy Award Nominated Director,
Prancer, Bang the Drum Slowly, The Looking Glass

Contents

Introduction

Arts maestro Harry Musselwhite has always been a conduit between Floyd County, Georgia, and the world at large, and his New Mexico columns continue that tradition.

From music to movies to fishing and food, his writings uncover the sometimes surprising, always fascinating, cultural parallels in “The Enchanted Land” and “The Land of Enchantment.”

During his more than three decades as a columnist for the *Rome News-Tribune* in Northwest Georgia, he’s shared his delight in both the elite and mundane beauty around us with fierce advocacy and a lively humor.

An early column in Rome, for example, chastises the tendency to fund athletics at the expense of the arts—and the early champion of the Rome International Film Festival is still writing about the value of the movie industry, to both the hearts and wallets of the city. But there’s also the thrill of his recent pilgrimage to Denver with his bride “to see the Rockies play our Atlanta Braves.”

Harry’s first dispatch from “Ranchero Musselwhite” drew on the similarities with his former hometown: the country living, a respect for horses, the recognition of Native American influences and neighbors’ dedication to yardwork. But differences will out, as New Mexico’s stunning lawns of cacti, succulents and stones reflect a scarcity of water.

“So to my friends and readers in Rome, Georgia, I say to you: love your rivers, grow less grass, explore your heritage, and love your animals.

“Now about those green chiles…”

The comparisons and contrasts come alive in his epistles. The borders between Georgia and Florida versus new and old Mexicos. Southern rocking chair porches and his portale in the Rio Grande Valley. A rare Waffle House in Albuquerque.

And always through the lens of a filmmaker, a music maker, an educated and talented observer with the ability to elevate the universality of the arts that can bind us to each other.

As Harry so aptly puts it in "Wonders of the World," a November 2021 column detailing outdoor vistas, architectural treasures and a dinner party where Rome native and internationally hailed mezzosoprano Jamie Barton was a topic of conversation:

"Whether through images of an antique truck, a church with an interesting history, an ancient mountain, or a famous opera singer with a local connection, our world is linked by images and sounds. We are connected by so many random happenstances no matter if many miles separate us."

Enjoy this volume of stories that so joyously blend the warmth of the Santa Ana winds with the comfort of the Coosa River. I sure did.

Diane Wagner
City Editor
Rome News-Tribune

Red or Green?

Does the State of Georgia have a "state question"? Well, believe it or not, New Mexico does: "Red or Green?"

The answer out here is "Christmas".

Chile season is early out here. I am not sure why, but it could be because we have had a robust monsoon season, and each evening, the magnificent southwestern thunderheads form and release a cooling and nurturing downfall. This I believe is good for the chile farmers' important work down Hatch, New Mexico, way.

When one orders enchiladas, tostadas, or burritos, the waitperson out here quickly asks, "Red or Green?" Hence, the state question.

I prefer Green Chile. Its distinct earthy flavor combined with just a perfect amount of fire gives lunch at one of my new haunts a spicy taste bomb. My son, the Georgia Tech phenom, prefers red chile, particularly at a great café named Teofilo's located at the center of my Village of Los Lunas.

If you wish both, you say, "Christmas". The cook then ladles half red and half green on your enchilada of choice, adds cheese, and one is ready to feast.

I love the hamburger up at Schroeder's North, just above Berry College. It is called the Samburger, after the great renaissance person Sam Edwards, who runs the great eatery. It is my favorite hamburger in the world.

If Sam ever decides to open up a Schroeder's in New Mexico (please, oh please!), he would have to offer a Samburger with a New Mexico twist: The Samburger Green Chile Cheeseburger. The Green Chile Cheeseburger is found at, well, every burger joint in the region.

The other day I went to a real working person's lunch spot, right on New Mexico Highway 47, called TJ's.

I sat at a table with a view of the train tracks leading north to Albuquerque and south to Belen. The New Mexico Railrunner Train races up and down this route throughout the day.

On this particular day at TJ's, I noted that I was the only Anglo fellow in the place. A rich tapestry of America's melting pot representing Native American and Latino cultures was seated all around me.

A striking elderly couple from the area sat next to me. They drank coffee with their green chile enchiladas. Wow!

I ordered my usual chicken enchiladas and responded to "the question" with "green". The plate arrived and I dug in.

As I began to enjoy the rich flavors of my lunch, an accompanying sensation came on like a Norman Arey opinion about the Georgia Bulldog offense.

Heat. Intense culinary heat. I began to sweat. My nose began to run. I had to ask for another paper napkin. This was serious.

My pride was at stake, for the room was full of New Mexicans who were, I supposed, used to this fire from Hatch, New Mexico. It was no time to wimp out, but I was in trouble. I reached for the squeeze bottle of honey found on all New Mexico tables, but that was a flag of defeat.

Just as I was about to give up, the elegant New Mexican lady leaned toward her husband's ear. I could just make out what she said.

"Dang, these chiles are hot today!"

Through my tears, I managed a smile, and I poured a huge dollop of honey on my sopapilla and calmed the heat in my mouth. If La Dona found the chiles hot that day, then by golly, they were, pride be hanged!

One last word about New Mexico food, and that word would be bacon. The world champion bacon provider lies about thirty minutes north of Rome, Georgia, and that place is the renowned Dirt Town Deli. Readers of this newspaper's editorial page are familiar with a cadre who swear by its food and its regulars, and bacon is its wonder, in my opinion.

I am not going to talk about a serving of bacon I enjoyed recently in Taos, New Mexico. I am not going to compare its crispness, its succulent flavor, or its perfect rust color to its Georgia relation. I am not going to name the café. That would be wrong, and it would betray my membership in the Dirt Town Literary Society.

I must blame my momentary betrayal on oxygen depravation, having been seated in the shadow of sacred Taos Mountain that dramatic morning.

But….

Now that I think about it, there is a culinary question for Rome, Georgia: "Schroeder's North or Schroeder's Downtown?" The answer, either way, is delightful.

July 2015

Ernie Pyle

My dad, Harry Sr., was a proud veteran of the United States Navy. He served on the Destroyer USS Cunningham in the Pacific until he was injured during the battle for Okinawa.

He didn't bring back much from the war besides crippling injuries to both lower legs. There were a few things in the basement that I discovered over my young years: a great kbar sheath knife, a captured Japanese rifle, and a wonderful olive drab field jacket that I wore during my college years.

A treasure I discovered one day in that dusty bin was a copy of illustrator and World War II writer Bill Mauldin's book *Up Front*. The writer of the introduction was America's most popular columnist Ernie Pyle.

I remember seeing a plaque commemorating Pyle at Indiana University during my studies there, but at that time I failed to make the connection with my dad's book in that Georgia basement.

My wife recently gave me a copy of Richard Melzer's book *Ernie Pyle in the American Southwest*, and I realized this was the Ernie Pyle whose words had taken me to the war that my dad and so many of my friends' relatives had fought.

Professor Melzer is a much-published retired member of the faculty at The University of New Mexico-Valencia, where my wife is the Dean.

Pyle was an established syndicated columnist before the outbreak of the war. He was beloved by American newspaper readers for his depictions of the regular folks he encountered in his journeys. He called himself "the constant voyager" in that he traveled the country near and far and created columns based on casual conversations noted in cafes, hotels, and farm stands. The public loved Ernie Pyle and his writing.

Pyle and his wife found themselves returning again and again to New Mexico. During Pyle's war years he would find natives of New Mexico in the European theatre and each would describe the purple sunsets, rouge mountains, and clear mountain air of The Land of Enchantment. The GI's would crowd around Pyle as he described his New Mexico and in turn they would be given a brief respite from the daily carnage they experienced.

Indeed Bill Mauldin was also a native of southern New Mexico, and he never understood why Pyle would want to live in the northern part of the state. Pyle would often give his soldier interviewees a Zippo lighter after a good story. The Zippo Company would ship Pyle cases of lighters so that he could share a device known for its reliability and its effectiveness in high winds.

By the end of the European conflict, Pyle was sick of the war, and wanted to return to Jerry and his home on Girard Avenue in Albuquerque. Many felt he was an important part of morale on the home front, and even Eleanor Roosevelt personally asked him to do for the men in the Pacific what he did for their European counterparts.

Even more troubling, the constant exposure to death began to wear him down, and Pyle began to have dramatic feelings about his own death. He was tired. His notoriety led to a lack of privacy. Even when he had brief respites in Albuquerque fans would drive to his home and ask to come in and be in the presence of a writer they claimed as one of their own.

Melzer writes: "Ernie Pyle was the thirtieth American war correspondent killed in World War II."

A sniper on Okinawa killed Pyle at the age of 44. The country reeled at the news that this columnist who had celebrated the common person could be taken from them so quickly and violently.

Last week I had a meeting in Albuquerque, and enjoyed my time with a colleague in an area near The University of New Mexico called Nob Hill. Girard Avenue runs north and south at the edge of the area, and I decided, like so many American fans, to visit Ernie Pyle's home.

I got turned around and couldn't decipher the instructions from my iPhone, but I remembered that when Ernie and Jerry bought their house, they wanted a view of the desert vistas from a higher elevation (now gone due to the sprawl of ABQ). I looked ahead and saw the avenue rise toward the south, and I drove forward.

I saw the sign first: The Ernie Pyle House/Library. I looked left and there it stood. To say that this house was modest is to make an understatement. This small abode, sitting on a peaceful corner, was the epitome of a common person.

I parked, crossed the street, and half expected Jerry Pyle to meet me at the door and say, "Sorry, Ernie's in England talking to the boys." Alas, the little library was closed, but I walked around the white clapboard house and peeked into the windows.

Of course now the building is full of books, but one can see the small kitchen, petite living room, and tiny bedroom where Ernie and Jerry spoke of their travels, their troubles, and the tormented world around them.

I don't know if there is a newspaper columnist in the country today with such a connection to the common person, but there was a day when almost every American knew the name and words of Ernie Pyle.

I sat on Ernie Pyle's porch for a few moments and thought about the power of words and newspapers and the joy of simplicity in life. I noted that the same pure and crafted simplicity exhibited by the various columnists of this newspaper is available daily. Ernie Pyle and his pal Bill Mauldin would be proud.

November 2015

Christmas Cards

My colleague in the *Rome News Tribune* columnist world, Severo Avila, was so generous in his ongoing Christmas card campaign. I say good for him, and even greater to those who sent in cards!

I am writing this a couple of weeks before the big December holiday, and I count seven Christmas cards on our holiday table and one of those yearly "what we've been up to for the last twelve months" letters.

First, about those letters: I read them. Every word. I have a natural curiosity about family and friends, and sometimes when one is separated by many miles, these letters "fill in the blanks".

Okay, secretly I hope to read from cousin Jim, "Well the covert operation in Belize didn't quite work out like we'd hoped. Casualties were at a minimum, and we rescued the ambassador's daughter after a brief firefight."

But no, what we all usually read goes something like "Disney World was a blast this year, and the great Disney nurses were able to stop Jonny's nosebleed in time for the 'It's a Small World' ride."

When I was a college student I always sent my voice teacher a Christmas Card, both in undergraduate and graduate schools. We all in our private music studios sent Christmas wishes to our teachers. We held our mentors in the highest esteem, and to receive a return card was a cause for celebration.

Back when I taught at Berry, the students rarely did such a thing. Sometimes at the end of the semester they would bring a small token to the office such as cookies or candy, but I never got Christmas cards from my musical flock.

Kathryn Nobles never failed, however. This talented pianist and master of Kindermusik would arrive at my door with a plate of delicious sweets, and they offered sustenance during the trying days of exams and music juries.

I keep in touch with folks from the banks of the Rio Grande here with the usual suspect: email. But I also send friends near and far cards that I find interesting. The art world in New Mexico is huge, and every gallery has a gift shop with interesting cards. I buy them and mail them to folks all over the country. I guess it's my way of staying connected to friends "back east".

I like the classic Christmas cards. As I look over at the seven lonely cards here, I see that two of the seven are the so-called photo cards with a montage of various poses from families on vacation.

I bet everyone who reads this column has a photo card featuring large families posed on beaches sporting white shirts and khakis. This seems to be a rite of passage for American families, and these photos are ubiquitous on Facebook.

I mailed a script this week from the Village of Los Lunas Post Office. The line was not too long, and it appeared that the villagers were all sending holiday packages to loved ones all over. I spied addresses in Delaware and Illinois, but alas, I did not spot any citizens with large stacks of Christmas cards in hand.

We were in Washington, DC, lately, and I spent a lovely day in The National Gallery of Art. This address is one of our nation's true treasures, and if you visit our capitol, plan at least a half day to revel in the world class collection of master art.

The gift shop at the National Gallery was filled with splendid collections of Christmas Cards. Many featured reproductions of art masterpieces in the museum, and I bought a couple of boxes to share. I think a card one can hold and examine is far superior to a quick iphone photo snap from a gallery.

There was a large variety of musical themed Christmas cards at The National Gallery gift shop, what with music being such an important aspect of the season. My personal favorite in this particular category are reproductions of renaissance paintings showing various lutes, wind instruments, and gatherings of madrigal singers.

I will go to the mailbox this afternoon with anticipation. I hope to receive a card from a former student, an old music colleague, or a beloved family member. If a long letter with an amusement park anecdote is in the mix, well, I will read it with pleasure.

So if you are of a mind, you will probably find boxes of Christmas cards at a huge discount this close to Christmas day. Grab a box, buy a sheet of stamps, locate your address book (remember those?) and send some love and affection out into the world courtesy of The United States Postal Service.

Oh yes. Don't forget. Peace on Earth and Goodwill to ALL People!

December 2016

San Lorenzo

The primitive road leading to San Lorenzo Canyon gives the term "washboard" a vivid new meaning. We drove approximately an hour south of our Village of Los Lunas, New Mexico, on speedy I-25, and we now faced a wilderness road that would guarantee a top speed of ten miles an hour. We figured a good half hour to our destination.

It mattered not.

On this beautiful Sunday morning, we packed water (an absolute requirement for hiking in New Mexico), sunscreen, safety necessities, and two very excited pups. We anticipated a day beneath the fabled mesas of central New Mexico.

Barely north of Socorro, New Mexico, we traveled along a two-lane road that featured a cattle crossing approximately every quarter mile. The sides of this road were dotted with folks living on this planet on their own terms. Out here they call it "Living off the Grid."

One outpost promised the sale of New Mexico honey. I wish we had stopped. Goats, sheep, lamas, donkeys, and rusted out hulks of abandoned school buses filled the junk-strewn compound. I would guess that forlorn destination could be the fodder of three Rome News Tribune columns, at least.

We turned onto the washboard road and our forward motion slowed to a bumpy crawl. The pups were alarmed as the truck shuddered above the rocky lane and we slowed to a creep. The wilderness ahead beckoned.

My wife remarked that although the dirt road revealed a good deal of traffic, trash was a no show. Beyond the edge of the road we were treated to a western vista. We couldn't see a single power line. I loved it.

Slowly a rocky mesa revealed itself as if announcing a scene out of a classic western movie. Our rough and winding road rapidly narrowed.

Why do we seek the empty, the vast, and the quiet? Perhaps we seek to experience the emotions our ancestors felt when they encountered new natural experiences those ages ago. The land here in New Mexico, while beautiful, is completely unforgiving. Flashfloods, all manner of prickly plants, and wild animals all compete to make humans uncomfortable. Yet beauty abounds.

Slowly the walls of San Lorenzo Canyon embraced us. Prehistoric rock formations leaned in as if inspecting our suitability for entrance. Each moment brought another stunning formation framed against our turquoise sky.

After a couple of slow canyon curves, the floor widened. We saw our first fellow humans in a while, a young couple strapping on backpacks. They gave us a friendly wave and then set out from their vehicle down a canyon trail

We parked next to an empty truck hitched to a livestock trailer. The pups whined in excitement, and we exited the truck with anticipation.

The quiet was deafening on the canyon floor. We instantly became attenuated to the natural sounds of the area as we set out. A screech of a low flying hawk echoed through the ancient stone walls.

We were completely alone. We hiked for a bit and the only sounds were the panting of the dogs and the scratch of rocky sand against our boots. Every few yards we stopped and took photos that certainly would be at home in National Geographic, or at least Facebook.

Every turn in the trail offered a view into ancient earth. I wondered if Spanish conquistadors experienced the same magic.

We turned back after a while, and the return portion of our hike provided even more visual delights. Becoming bolder, the pups scrambled up some low setting rock formations, both dogs straining against their leashes.

Back at our parking spot we refreshed ourselves with water still cold in our modern water containers. The pups were even more thirsty than we humans and they lapped until they were content.

Filled with peace, we exited the sacred land. It was as if the bride and myself had been rejuvenated down to the cellular level. A bit of motion high on the canyon wall caught my eye, and there stood a bighorn sheep watching from her safe distance.

As we rounded a curve on the way out a posse of riders cheerfully greeted us. A family, owners of the stock trailer, was enjoying a Sunday trail ride. They all waved and we returned the greeting. Bringing up the rear was a child, no more than six or seven years old, guiding his paint pony behind the grownups.

We stopped one more time before returning to the paved road. A slight rise in the desert afforded a spectacular view that demanded a pause. We could see from our desert vantage point all the way across the Rio Grande Valley and out to mountains in the east. The angle prevented any 21st Century visual intrusion. Even the pups grew quiet.

I'm going back soon. My soul requires it. I hope you find your quiet canyon no matter where you live.

April, 2019

Water Water Everywhere

The snow-capped Sangre de Christo Mountains towering above Santa Fe were one of the first things I noticed upon my second trip to New Mexico in the summer of 1980. I remember making my first drive out to the opera house and looking north. "Don't see many snow capped peaks in Georgia," I remarked to the driver.

The management of the Santa Fe Opera immediately impressed on their young vocal charges the importance of hydration. It's dry in New Mexico, and one notices the lack of humidity immediately.

I didn't realize until many years later the importance of those snow peaked mountains. I now know the snow equals life.

Around two weeks ago my bride woke me up with a lovely little phrase, "No water!" The faucets made rattling sounds but gave no water. Bad sign this, especially since it was a Saturday morning in the middle of a three-day holiday weekend.

Here at Ranchero Musselwhite we use a well, and in the few years we've been here, thankfully, the water flow has been consistent.

We went to the control unit conveniently located at floor level behind our washer dryer. After muscling the appliances out of the way, the space proved too small for my gorilla-sized frame, so the bride squeezed in with flashlight in hand.

No amount of button pushing, fuse box resetting, or stern verbal challenges would make the control unit spring to life. No water, no shower, no instantly refilled toilet tanks, and no dishwasher would accompany our holiday weekend.

We combed our hair, put on baseball caps, and made the drive of shame to one of the local big box retailers. The big stores here have whole aisles of water that vary from personal sizes to multi-gallon plastic jugs. We purchased several of the XXL's and a few of the smaller sizes, for we knew that it was going to be a long weekend.

Our life saver neighbor, Mr. Bob, came through again for he had an elevated spigot situated at the back of his property that allowed easy access for the pickup truck, and we were able to refill the plastic jugs throughout the dry ordeal.

In the meantime, word came that local authorities had closed the hiking trails that line the famed Rio Grande. The reason being that this year we had so much snow up on the mountains with the resultant melt-off that the mighty river, often a trickle, flows like its sister to the east, The Mighty Mississippi. The acequias, or the "ditches" as they call them out here, are full and giving the big alfalfa fields south of here a fantastic spring soaking. The pepper farmers even more south in Hatch must be doing a happy dance after the previous several years of drought.

So ironic, but there was no laughter in the casa, when we had no water, and a mile east a famous river was overflowing.

Rome, Georgia, and the state had a wet spring according to all reports. Now, the State of Georgia is in the middle of a drought. Truly feast or famine as the old sages wrote.

Ah the joys of what my Aunt Dorine called "A French Bath." Heating water on the stove, placing in a bowl, carrying to the shower, mixing with cold water from a plastic jug, and then, voila, two minutes later, a refreshing cleansing bath. This is not my idea of getting ready for the prom.

Tuesday morning I made the call promptly at eight a.m. to the well company, and two very nice men arrived approximately forty minutes later. I expected a quick reset from a magical, yet hidden, reset button, but more testing commenced. The pump was okay. Hurray! The control unit was not. Cue Wagnerian tubas.

After a quick trip back to HQ, by lunch we had a brand new well control unit, and all for the bargain price of...wait for it... one thousand dollars. Ouchius Maximus.

It is with a wry smile that I tell you that as I write this, a huge thunderstorm is dumping water on my house, the adjacent orchard, and the huge alfalfa field out my living room window. To this, I give thanks.

The newspaper in Albuquerque reports that the farmers around me are all in great moods because their crops are doing the backstroke in life giving water. The bird population seems particularly active this spring, and I know for sure they are not going thirsty.

If someone had called me in the middle of our long dry weekend and breathlessly offered, "Water for a thousand dollars?" Well...all I know is that first shower felt like a million dollars.

"I will do water – beautiful, blue water." – Claude Monet

June, 2019

Auto Dealerships in the Morning

I arrived at the auto dealership just after eight in the morning in order to present my wife's new SUV for some minor adjustments. The uniformed attendants greeted me warmly and I asked for directions to a nearby breakfast joint.

I was immediately given directions to yet another dealership. Pardon me, for I was skeptical. What? Walk down the street to the Ford dealership?

The name of the grill was featured, marquee style, on the side of the building next to the famous trademark of the American automobile icon. "The Mustang Café" was highly recommended by the folks down at the Subaru dealership.

I entered and found a 1960's style drive-in complete with checkered tile, chrome stools, and "Happy Days" style decorations. I approached the counter, grabbed a menu, and ordered New Mexico style huevos rancheros complete with green chile. Remember, readers, I am in the middle of a lot filled with Ford F-150's, Mustangs, and more.

How was it? My eggs were cooked to perfection and they swam the backstroke in a most agreeable pool of fresh New Mexico Green Chile, just spicy enough to be interesting. The coffee was roadside diner perfect.

I noticed several years ago that auto dealerships changed from the grungy mismatched furniture dens of yore to more of a patron pleasing experience. My bride had purchased an Audi two-seater and we were required to drive down to North Atlanta for regular service appointments.

I was shocked upon entering the lobby to find I had my choice of designer coffee drinks while waiting. Cappuccinos, lattes, and more were available to sip while watching large screen televisions. One could also purchase a vehicle if so moved.

I am writing this while sitting in the waiting area of an Albuquerque Subaru dealership. The faux leather designer chairs are comfortable. Around the corner is an area suitable for laptop work with wall sockets arranged for easy access. Coffee and fresh cookies are available. The entire area is tastefully decorated with vintage Santa Fe Opera posters.

Screech!!!! (The sound of brakes) Opera posters? In a car dealership? All the opera posters are displayed in matching gunmetal grey frames. Did I mention the parquet wooden floors?

Wait, there's more.

In the men's room there is a framed AND autographed poster by a well-known New Mexico artist. Not just a nobody artist, but the poster features the kind of art that shows in Santa Fe galleries and New York showcases.

Oh, they sell cars here, too.

Somebody stop me!

Oh no dear readers, the coffee table next to me is not stacked with old copies of "Car and Driver" magazine. Only the most current issue of "GQ Magazine" is good enough for ABQ Subaru, and how comforting it is to be able to compare one's attire with actor Seth Rogan while scoping out the 2019 Forrester. The Wall Street Journal is available for the latest business intel.

So here I sit. I half expect someone to appear and ask if I would enjoy a relaxing foot massage. I hope the hot tub temperature is just right.

Just down the street is the Dodge Ram dealership, my current favorite vehicle. I am so tempted to walk down and see what delights might be in store. Perhaps they have an indoor arena and I can watch team roping or bronc riding. Would it be too much to anticipate a singer performing King George Strait's greatest hits for the truck buying public?

Certainly Dodge Ram should consider a combination truck dealership and steakhouse. I think it would be a huge hit to tuck into a rib eye while getting one's oil changed.

Over at the Range Rover dealership they could have champagne and oysters at the ready and liveried English butlers describing the latest developments in rear camera technology.

Now I know my brother Mike Ford right in Rome, Georgia, is reading this and shaking his head. I know the coffee in his coffee pot can easily be labeled vintage, but Mike, maybe a couple of doilies on the chairs? Just kidding, I like you the way you are at Mike Ford Auto.

Happy auto shopping, dear readers, and please remember that coat and tie are optional. Reservations only, please.

June, 2019

New Guitar

I needed a cable for my home recording studio so I drove up to Albuquerque to the Home Depot of music stores, Guitar Center. Remember the sign in the music store featured in "Wayne's World?"

It read something like "No Stairway to Heaven!"

That's sort of what a visit to Guitar Center is like. The electric guitar area of the mega-store is populated by what are known as "shredders" who play many notes fast and loud. Saturday mornings at Guitar Center are especially dangerous because that's when all the kids show up to try out new guitar shaped objects.

I initially avoided the guitar area and strode purposefully to the recording area. If one's wits are lacking, this can be a very perplexing area. There were cables of every length and purpose. I stood mute before the huge display for quite a while. Purchasing an incorrect cable would mean another round trip up to the northeast side of ABQ, and I'd rather not.

I located my cable and brought two lengths to the nice young man at the counter. If I were casting a movie about a rock star, I would definitely want this gentleman's headshot. He sported long black hair and just enough facial fauna to maintain his street cred. I bet he can shred.

Dude Man confirmed that I was about to purchase the correct cable, and I realized I had some free time on my hands. I decided to browse, to look around, and to see what I could see. Uh oh.

This could be a wife's worst nightmare: a husband roaming free through a guitar store.

I spied a pair of studio headphones that, honestly, I needed the next day in order to record properly a guest for our (with Donald J. Davenport) podcast "The Dungball Express." They were priced right and they quickly landed on the counter next to my two cable packages.

I then went over to the modest printed music area, and to my delight I found a complete collection of the music of Steely Dan. It was a bit dear, but it landed next to the headphones and cables. Now I was rocking.

Closer and closer I drew until I stood trembling in the middle of the electric guitar area. On three points of the compass hung every style of guitar imaginable and two stories high. I guess I exuded a certain guitar gravitas, for I was greeted by the usually aggressive sales folks with a respectful, "Good afternoon, sir."

I admired a few instruments and then walked into the hermetically sealed acoustic guitar room. Yes, readers, they place all the acoustic guitars in a temperature and humidity controlled room bathed in soft lighting. My olfactory senses were very pleasantly assaulted. Seriously. This room REALLY smelled good.

It was at that moment that I spotted him. My heart melted.

He looked to be about ten. Dark brown unruly curls that rarely see a brush framed his angelic face. A young woman, who I took to be his mom, stood respectfully by. I pretended to examine a nearby guitar, but my attention was drawn to this developing scene.

The boy gazed at guitars hanging on the bottom row. Guitar Center displays their least expensive instruments closer to the ground. The Martins and Taylors hang way up high and require a sales person's assistance in order to audition.

The boy nervously took a guitar and held it close. I don't know if he could play, for I never saw him place fingers on the fretboard or strum the six strings. I do know that he held the instrument as if it were a brand new baby sister. The look on his face was out of this world.

Finally the boy turned to his mother and, with an almost imperceptible nod, signaled that this was the one.

Mom offered just a few words that were so soft and loving I couldn't make out among the din of other guitar sounds in the room. If the boy's face could light up more, well, I couldn't say.

Perhaps the tears in my eyes clouded my vision as I watched the mom open the door to the room and walk out to the register with what, if I may hazard a guess, may be a possession that may very well change a life.

Ask Rome's Scott Thompson about his first guitar. Ask David Bell during one of his breaks at a Rome watering hole about his first guitar.

I would wager they won't answer with "Hmmm, I can't seem to remember that first one."

So this afternoon when the school bus arrives at a modest Albuquerque neighborhood, a young man will race back to his room and slide a black case from under his bed. He'll notice that new guitar smell as he gently opens the case and takes out his instrument. He'll sit on the edge of the bed and carefully place his fingers on the neck and form a chord.

Lastly he'll look across the room at a mirror and see himself cradling his musical treasure.

He'll smile a smile that launches a whole new life.

November 2019

The Roadrunner

One of the first house warming gifts we received upon our move to New Mexico was a splendid watercolor of a roadrunner. My aunt Iris Musselwhite is a talented painter, and she wanted us to have a place appropriate piece of art for our new home.

I have many opportunities to photograph the majestic creature and because of social media law I am required to post these photos on Facebook. It only takes a moment or two for Rome's John Schroeder to post the familiar Warner Brothers vocalization of the road runner: "Meep, Meep!"

How iconic is the roadrunner?

Well, our New Mexico commuter rail system is named the Rail Runner and is painted like a roadrunner in full speed posture. We have the Roadrunner Food Bank, Roadrunner Cash (The New Mexico Lottery), Roadrunner Auctions, and many more.

My discerning eye fails me when it comes to really finding the difference in these feathery creatures that crisscross my property. I do know that there are definitely two roadrunners in residence because one is skinny and sleek and the other is a bit rotund. Perhaps number two is a more skillful hunter, but my uneducated observation is that the food source is pretty consistent around Ranchero Musselwhite. Therefore I cannot explain the body difference.

The other morning I let my two pups, Roshi and Punkin', out for a walk. I heard quite a kerfuffle and moments, maybe seconds, later a grey/black streak blazed right by me. Two pups were in hot pursuit.

Tubby, as I shall call her/him, made a supreme tactical decision, and took flight. Landing on my slanted metal roof, the bird peered haughtily down at the two very confused dogs. I swear I heard a "Meep, Meep!"

There would have been no surprise if an anvil from the Acme Company had landed dramatically from my roof.

I have never seen a coyote chase a roadrunner out here. Both creatures are pretty fleet of foot, with the roadrunner by a nod due to its skillful use of trees, shrubs, and thorny bushes for defense and camouflage.

Nor do I see products from the famous Warner Brothers cartoon world known to all as The Acme Company.

I always chuckle when I hear someone mention Acme. I respond with, "Well, do you know that I know and worked with Marvin Acme?"

What you say?

The brilliant comedic actor Stubby Kaye portrayed Marvin Acme in the film *Who Shot Jessica Rabbit*. Acme was in love with the animated heroine and visited her nightclub every night.

The late Stubby Kaye and I acted together in a production of *Oklahoma* at St. Louis Muny Opera and we became fast friends. I never asked him if he had done any background research on either coyotes or roadrunners.

I stepped back in the shadows to see what the aforementioned roadrunner was going to do once the pups gave up hope of capture.

After a few moments, the creature hopped over to the roof's edge and sailed down with aerodynamic grace. The bird then ran quickly over to a tree line that edges our property and disappeared into the brush. I quickly followed.

"Where do they go?" I wondered.

The roadrunner is colored so magnificently that it effectively blends into the flora. I stared for quite a while and I could not find a feather in sight. I turned to go back to my house when a quick visual memory registered. I spun around and there, sitting in a "V" formed by two branches, sat my little friend.

Upon landing, the roadrunner spread his/her wings creating a perfect fan shape that nine times out of ten would be mistaken for a pile of leaves, suspended over the ranch's surface. The bird so skillfully arrayed itself that I could not make out eyes, beak, or tail feathers.

I ran back to the house and grabbed my Nikon and a zoom lens. The roadrunner was in the same place upon my return and I delighted in getting several outstanding shots of this creature's unusual nesting choice.

The term "spirit animal" is used a lot out here. I would have to say my spirit animal has to be the amazing roadrunner.

Meep, meep, ya'll.

January 2020

The Ditch

With the majority (hopefully) of us sheltering perhaps it is a good time to share a bit of the New Mexico landscape that stretches before and behind Ranchero Musselwhite. I offer this as one way to take a little trip away from your confinement, if only in your mind.

I've written a tiny bit in this space about the irrigation phenomenon that we call the "acequia" or more locally, "the ditch." These waterways that spread like spider webs from our mother Rio Grande create an agricultural space south of Albuquerque. The water from "the ditch" nourishes vast fields of alfalfa, like the one in front of our home.

Your basic acequia is around six feet wide and, when running, the water is around three to five feet deep. Every quarter mile or so is a valve that farmers rotate in order to divert the water to their fields. This entails lots of rules, traditions, and strict laws. Out here they say, "Water is life."

On both sides of the acequia one finds a sandy road with room for one vehicle going either north or south. I've driven down one side of our nearby "ditch" and never encountered an oncoming car or truck. I guess one of us would back up until a widening or vacant driveway presented itself.

With the quarantine in place, my bride and I find great solace in a walk along the acequia. We put our two pups Roshi and Punkin' on leashes and off we go.

To the north we head toward the border of the Isleta Pueblo. The pups have a friend in a small Pueblo dog who monthly miraculously finds her way from the Pueblo to our yard. The three dogs play chase, strut about, and then the Pueblo dog races up to the acequia and runs back to Isleta. We hope to see where the dog lives on our walks, but the pup has not presented herself. Nevertheless, our two pups have tons of things to sniff as we walk the sandy way.

To the south we encounter the back areas of a wide variety of homes. One family has what looks like an armored compound made with twenty-foot long tin sheets. Two very fierce looking dogs who take great umbrage in our two pups walking near their home always announce our presence on the other side of the "ditch." We've never spotted any humans nor heard any human noises emanating from the compound.

We soon arrive at the border of the old Sichler Farm, the ancestral home of our friends The Dollahites. Thomas Dollahite is a way cool farmer/philosopher who had the good graces to establish a European style coffeehouse at the edge of our near-by highway. From the vantage point of the acequia, we see his parents' home with their large solar panel array and green fields dotted with cows chewing and well, chewing.

As we cross a small bridge leading into the Dollahite property, a large watergate similar to ones we've seen in rural France sits in the acequia. The water rushes through with zen-like gurgling, and we always pause and quietly observe the rushing water.

We continue south and see all manner of residences. Of particular note, many homes feature parked recreational vehicles. New Mexicans love to get out into the magnificent land here, and many homes are graced with a large RV ready for the weekend.

So far we have not seen any fellow walkers on the acequia. Yesterday we saw a couple stacking firewood beside their adobe home. The gentleman sported a long braided ponytail that stretched all the way to his waist. Upon sensing our presence, both straightened up and gave a wave.

Other than yard dogs, we've yet to encounter any larger animal life. Here we all know that the acequia is basically the New Mexico interstate system for coyotes. We've not seen the animals, but there are plenty of tracks to behold.

The architecture along the acequia ranges from early cement block to stunning adobe structures.

At the long end of our southern hike, a magnificent Tuscan-style home dominates the horizon. I walked past it once and two very large dogs dominated the exquisitely manicured grounds. They regarded me silently as I meandered by, and I had no wish to arouse their interest.

We turn back north with the pups' tongues hanging out. As one might guess the humidity here is basically non-existent, and the pups pull at their leashes in anticipation of their water bowl back at the ranchero.

The gurgle of the acequia, the wind rushing through the cottonwoods, the screech of our numerous red tailed hawks, and more provide a soothing soundtrack, and better yet, these sounds don't come from a computer speaker.

Whether your walk is by the Coosa River, a farm pond, or just around the neighborhood, keep a safe distance, wave, don't shake hands, and find your special mental hygiene spot. Peace.

April 2020

Dogs and Cats

Are you a dog person or a cat person? Both?

By necessity, I am a dog person, for cats stir up my allergies like nothing else on the planet. Dogs have no affect on my sensitive sinuses.

I have written of our two ranch dogs, Punkin' (female) and Roshi (male). They are affectionate, loyal, and enjoy cruising our New Mexico property. For the most part, however, they stay indoors. In front of one of our large front facing windows sits a love seat, and the two pups love to sit at the top of the cushions and survey their baronial kingdom.

Nowadays this consists of randomly barking at the cows that have recently come to join us. The cows regard them with heavy lidded contempt, and I am not sure as to what purpose the pups are barking.

Are they saying, "Get off my lawn?" Well, "lawn" being a euphemism, in that in New Mexico it would probably more accurate to shout "Get off my sand/rocks!"

Are they announcing, "Hey folks, there are large hooved creatures just steps from our front door?"

Eventually they tire of taunting the animals. They come back inside, get a drink of water, and take a nap.

The two pups are the first canines that we have felt the need to take to a groomer. I would describe our animals as medium haired, in that my amateur call is that the two have medium length hair.

The New Mexico sun can be brutal, and we like to keep the two trimmed for the late spring through the end of fall, but our groomer has been closed due to the Quarantine.

So we ordered some clippers.

I own my own set of clippers due to the fact that I've sported facial hair for decades, and I am not interested in the "Brooklyn Beard" look. That being said, I have a certain familiarity with clippers.

My bride, the dean, took the lead and trimmed Roshi first.

I guess they were used to their regularly scheduled visits to the groomer, for the pups sat quietly during the process. We trimmed one dog on one day and then the other the next.

Well. The good news and the not so good news:

Their hair is definitely trimmed, and we feel that their comfort level is way up the chart. They don't seem to be panting so hard and they are running around in their usual frisky way.

The bad news? If one used a weed wacker on an animal with no harm to said pup's health, that is what our pups look like. I know it was our first time, and that the dogs are cooler, but aesthetically, they appear perhaps as a dog imagined by Juan Miro.

For Punkin', the hairier of the two, the pile of fur left in the wake of her cutting was equal to the actual dog. We are going to attempt a second session to give a bit of finesse to the cut, but wowza, the results!

Several folks on social media have asked for pictures of the recently shorn Roshi and Punkin'.

Not a chance.

Other social media pals have indicated that they studied YouTube videos of pet trimming and attempted to replicate. Our friends have noted limited success and several abject failures.

So this beautiful New Mexico morning Roshi and Punkin' are napping peacefully on the back of the sofa. They harbor no ill feelings at all. They know that their debut at the Westminster Kennel Show is a non-starter.

We will get better at the business of puppy trimming. I guess.

In the meantime, I noticed my shadow while outside this morning. It appeared that there was all manner of hair sticking out at strange angles from my head.

Oh lordy, I think the bride is going to have to grab the human clippers.

Do not stay tuned for pictures.
Stay safe and sane.

May 2020

Pecos Zen

I write this morning nestled in the bosom of the beautiful Pecos Valley, New Mexico. Flowing approximately twenty-five yards from this keyboard is the crystalline Pecos River. More about that later.

The bride and I decided to get away for a few days, and we called it a "mental hygiene getaway." I suggested a cabin up on the Pecos where we would still be quarantined but surrounded by some spectacular New Mexico nature.

Pecos is an old mining area. Abandoned villages, once thriving, line the Pecos River as it winds down from the eastern side of the Sangre de Christos Mountains. The road that parallels the river at times dwindles down to almost one lane. There are handsome million dollar movie star compounds hidden behind thick trees, and there are "off the grid" folks who have patched together combinations of trailers, containers, and lean-to's.

Famous movie star Greer Garson and her cattle baron husband bought a huge ranch near here many years ago, and actor Val Kilmer ("I'm your huckleberry!") eventually purchased the sprawling property. Jane Fonda also built a ranch here, but both Kilmer and Fonda have sold their retreats to anonymous buyers. Rich anonymous buyers.

Most of the dwellings up here are decidedly modest in keeping with a common theme of "getting away from the rat race." The house we are renting is a traditional adobe New Mexican with tile floors that are deliciously cool to our bare feet.

The owner built a small wooden deck at the edge of the Pecos and that is where my bride sits and watches me fly fish in the chilly waters. The river is clean and flowing and we had a great time last night drinking adult beverages and watching the very active bird population dive bomb the evening insect population hovering over the river.

A neighbor briefly made an appearance sitting on a large rock a few yards to our west. He had some sort of portable music player and sat listening to Latino music. I wondered why the sounds of this magnificent river gurgling and splashing over shoals did not provide the man enough of a soundtrack. He listened for a bit longer, and then silently disappeared into the brush adjacent to the river. The man owns two large and fierce dogs that run down with growls and barks and then retreat with wagging tails. I am hoping that there will be no interaction with our two pups who take great umbrage in these dogs inspecting our yard.

Vehicles belonging to trout enthusiasts dot the road north out of Pecos Village. Several outdoor sports enthusiasts emerged from vehicles in full trout fishing regalia: boonie hats, Orvis vests, expensive fly rods, sun-repellant shirts, and suitable footwear.

My fellow trout fishermen in Floyd County, John Graham (currently on the Yellowstone River), Scott Thompson, and John Kirkland, know that trout have eyes on the back of their heads and that one literally has to sneak up on the river in order to have a chance. So far, my score is trout: 10 and Harry: 0.

Would you like to know how much it matters? Not a bit.

My son-in-law, great band director Eric Thompson, sent me a text from Kansas State University country yesterday.

"Are you fishing or catching?"

So far, just fishing. You see, the Zen of that weighted line, the balletic arc of the fly rod, and the joy of placing that fly just so is to be connected with something profound. A perfect cast feels like a perfectly placed vocal note in opera. It is akin to an out of body experience, yet the rod and line are clearly in one's control. The experience is a step toward excellent mental hygiene.

The elevation here is high, over 7,000 feet above sea level. That means that the area is conducive for the propagation of one of my favorite species, the Aspen tree.

I love the white bark usually scarred with various natural designs. Sometimes one can imagine a face carved into the trunk of the tree. However, the best part of finding a stand of Aspens is when the wind moves through the heart shaped leaves and produces an amazing shimmering sound. If fairies designed wind chimes, they would sound like Aspen leaves in the wind.

I will head out on the river in a bit. If I bring home some trout to fry, all the better, but none required to define a great day. I'll listen for the counterpoint of the Pecos River and the chimes of the Aspen trees. I'll send my peaceful Zen to the kind folks of Floyd County, Georgia.

July 2020

The Lost Highway

"I have never been lost, but I will admit to being confused for several weeks." – Daniel Boone

"Not all those who wander are lost." – J.R.R.Tolkien

We pulled the noisy Ford Econoline van onto I-25 South, and pointed our nose toward Socorro, NM. The van was the property of The University of New Mexico, and that meant for this day's journey I would be passenger, narrator, and second navigator on call.

Normally, for some unexplained reason, I usually drive when we head south. This day I had the great pleasure of looking out the window and observing splendid southwestern scenery. What a treat it turned out to be.

We've had great rain, so the huge orchards that line the road at Belen, New Mexico, were green, tall, and proud. The vast arboreal operation was planted with geographic precision, and as we raced by I wondered what kind of wildlife lived in such an imposing and formal stand of trees.

We quickly passed the orchard and brown mesas immediately loomed to the west. To the east, the verdant Rio Grande Valley snaked southward as far as the eye could see.

Our destination? Somewhere near the tiny spot on the New Mexico map called Datil. Folks around here pronounce it "Day – Till." I have no further information on said hamlet.

Our mission? We were to meet one of my wife's art professors at the home of an artist who soon will move to Portugal. The painter donated seventy pieces of her work that range in size from several inches to several feet. We were locked in with one of those map applications on our phone, and all seemed good.

At Socorro, New Mexico, we turned west. The interstate faded instantly into a two-lane country road. The road sign read

"Datil, 64 Miles."

The big attraction on this rural highway was featured in a major Hollywood film entitled "Contact." It starred Jody Foster and it concerns contact with alien beings through the use of the VLA.

In a sprawling valley on both sides of the highway sit huge radio telescopes that are so big they move about the valley on railroad tracks. The VLA stands for "Very Large Array."

We moved out of the valley and noticed one thing immediately. Our cell signal was zero. What we didn't know was (and we were guessing) that the loss of the signal seemed to have re-routed the directions to our artist's home.

Just to the south of Datil, we obeyed the phone (why it was still generating instructions remains a mystery) and turned onto one of the rockiest and awfully forlorn roads ever. The van moaned and groaned as we crept for well over a half an hour at a maximum speed of four miles per hour.

Our spines rattled with each buried boulder we crossed.

Suddenly we were brought up short. The road simply ended. There was a homestead sitting on a bluff above us, but there was no way I was going up there and ask for a cup of tea.

We spotted a forbidding trail to the right and turned onto it.

It's now going to get a little weird.

Before we could orient ourselves, a gentleman who appeared to have just arrived from a market in Katmandu burst upon the trail. He sat tall on an ATV and pulled up amid a cloud of dust and rocks. You might want to read that last sentence again.

He was dressed in white gauze from head to ankle (no shoes, right.) and he stopped at the van's side. A van, mind you, emblazoned with University of New Mexico logos.

He was curt. My wife informed him that we were a bit turned around.

He snarled, "What are you doing here?"

My unflappable wife responded, "We are here to pick up some art!"

That response rendered the pilgrim from the ancient east speechless for a moment. We told him our artist's name and didn't receive much of a response. He sort of told us to turn around and go back to the highway. So we did.

More spine shaking.

We spotted a Purina Feed sign on a fence with additional information: "Datil Feed." The hours on the sign indicated they were open. A feed store in the middle of nowhere? It was too late to second guess.

The wife nosed the van slowly into a compound and we rounded a small turn. Three cowboys, two male and one female, greeted us. Two standing and one sitting in an ATV. Does everyone in rural New Mexico have an ATV?

The female of the trio, a cowgirl if you will, listened to our narrative and declared, "You are really lost!"

Directions were given. Yet another winding rocky road was in our immediate future, and at the end, a very worried painter greeted us with joy and a delicious lunch in the middle of nowhere.

The art was delivered to the University. The van was returned.

We have returned home, but I am still not sure where we went.

July 2020

Anticipation

There's a Carly Simon song called "Anticipation." Years ago Madison Avenue used the tune to market a popular brand of catsup. The song plays while images depicting the frustrating wait for a rich condiment to emerge, lava-like, from a bottle.

It may be a universal truth that we humans dislike anticipation.

This past week I suffered through a major bout of uncomfortable anticipation. My brother in music and life, David Johnson, took a trip with his wife Susan to a remote mountain retreat in West Virginia. The place was so removed that Internet and phone service was non-existent.

I talk to David every other night. Ours is a decades long friendship. I was the best man in his wedding, and he was the best man in mine. He is the godfather to my son.

I somehow forgot the actual calendar plans of his trip north, and I made my usual evening call. I encountered his familiar voice message, and knew that he would call back pretty quickly after finding a moment. The night passed and I mentioned to my more than wise wife that my friend had not called back.

"I bet they are on that trip to West Virginia," she replied.

I thought, well, he will call in the morning. A night of anticipation gently passed.

I waited for a decent window of opportunity to call again the next morning. Again I was greeted with the familiar voice mail. My anticipation meter rose. I texted. He always texts back within moments. I called his wife. Voice mail. I texted her. No response. By the end of the day, my anticipation level was reaching defcon 3.

"You know they may be in a mountain hollow in West Virginia with no Internet," said my wife.

I responded, “It’s 2020. Internet is everywhere.”

I spent the third day in a funk. Were they wrecked in a canyon off some north Georgia two-lane? Had a manure truck upended them? Anticipation.

The phone rang early on the fourth day.

A deep baritone voice said, “Hey.”

I replied, “I thought you moved.”

David laughed and said that they were way off the communications grid, and that with them were several high profile West Virginia business folks who were very frustrated about the lack of 21st century communications.

“But the food was terrific,” said David.

Anticipation.

A week earlier the text bell went off very early.

A certain young couple, let’s call them my children, were on the way to the hospital to deliver Mr. Henry Michael Thompson. The notice of the impending arrival of our first grandchild pleasantly jolted us.

All through the morning the miracle of text messages and phone cameras kept us apprised of the new mom’s condition. With each “ping” we would receive pictures of the glowing mom (with her mask on) sitting in the maternity bed. We could not be there due to quarantine world, but it was the next best thing.

Then nothing. No text. No pics. No calls.

Anticipation.

I began to pace. Remember those old cartoons of expectant fathers pacing outside the maternity ward, usually puffing frantically on a cigarette? Well, gentle readers, that was me, sans tobacco.

My wife is like the Rock of Gibraltar, yet I could see her eyes were wide open with anticipatory stress. Outwardly she remained calm, unlike me. I knew she was worried as one hour morphed into two.

I had an old chair that had met the end of its days out in the carport, and I went out and took my stress to bear on the creaky relic. I made short work of the demolition. My heart was not into the task but my body appreciated the activity.

Anticipation. More pacing.

Ah, a text "ping" came through. It was David and Susan Johnson.

"Have you heard anything?" queried David.

"Not yet," I hastily replied.

I thought I was going to explode. My imagination ran wild as I pondered things that should not be pondered. My baby girl and her magnificent husband were eleven hours away, and all I could offer were loving sentiments and sweaty pacing.

Another hour went by and we were at anticipation defcon one thousand.

We both leapt at the phone as we heard the "ping".

A new human being had just made his entrance on planet Earth.

Blood pressure back down, we poured champagne and toasted our first grandchild. We gave thanks for the health and safety of all concerned.

Anticipation.

Sometimes it's worth the wait.

August 2020

A Stickie Situation

It is said that there's no such thing as a free lunch. However, I receive free return address stickers without asking.

I just got back from the mailbox and brought in a large envelope with official phrases stamped thereon like "Official Documents Enclosed" and "Secret Nuclear Codes Included." Okay, I jest about the latter.

I believe the United Postal Service is one of our nation's treasures, right up there with the National Park Service.

Not too long ago I started receiving requests for donations for a wide variety of good causes. Missives entreated me to save the ducks, sponsor poor villages in foreign countries, and today's communication indicated I was in sore need of additional life insurance.

The common thread in these queries is that they are accompanied by a sheet self-sticking return address labels.

Some good thought has gone into the design of these labels. A number feature the first letter of my last name rendered in a font worthy of a French jewelry designer. Others have, albeit small, lovely photos of Labrador Retrievers bounding through marshland. Today's sheet featured my name and address in four separate styles.

Several label rows sported a handsome gothic 'M' and as usually the case there is the oft-used American flag.

I feel this free stickie movement is a relatively new one. I wonder what scenario birthed this phenomenon. Did the brain trust exclaim, "Let's give 'em free address labels. They'll HAVE to donate to our save the mollusks campaign!"

Perhaps it's too simplistic, but are we to feel guilty accepting the free stickies and not donating money to the stated cause? It clearly must be very cheap to produce these sheets so there is no equal value clause here to ponder.

I admit I am using the free stickies without any response on my part. The stickies arrive unbidden so I'm pretty guilt free on this. Besides, the parties I do support do not feel the need to offer these cheap, but appreciated, freebies.

Perhaps a larger issue here is that these entities are vicariously encouraging the experience of sending mail. The return address occupies its historic upper left hand corner of one's envelope unless one decides to turn the envelope over and center it over the flap.

When the free stickies first started arriving, I would affix them to bills. I wonder how many of my readers still use the mail for their monthly bills, given that most of my bills nowadays are paid electronically. Easy peasy.

I can remember my mom and dad sitting at the dining room table with stacks of paper and envelopes navigating the sometimes tough decisions concerning family finances during the 1960's. Upon completing their duties, there would always be a small stack of envelopes that I would run up to the mailbox, stick in, and raise the red flag.

I get letters from a small circle of correspondents. Rome musician Kenneth Moyers writes to me on what appears to be a vintage typewriter, and his notable script on the envelope announces his letter that I read immediately.

The late Dr. Ouida Dickey, Berry College legend and treasure, was always quick to respond to my letters. She addressed her letters with a flowing script and the upper left hand corner sported a classy self-stick return address label. Her letters were always filled with joy and positivism. I miss her.

Some elderly folks I write never respond. However, their children inform me that my letters are read over and over with much joy.

I salute you non-profits and insurance companies who provide me with a palette of return address labels. Even though I type my letters on the computer and print out the text, I still hand address the envelopes. Other than my signature, I feel it is important for the recipient to know that an actual human being touched pen to paper or envelope.

The other great use for the labels is for putting one's return address on Christmas Cards. Remember those?

Thanks United States Postal Service. Thank you for the letters, the magazines, and even the free return address stickies. We appreciate you and despite the wonders of the internet, we want you to thrive and last as long as our Republic.

August 26, 2020

My Grass is Blue

There is a Gary Larson cartoon that is entitled, "A Conductor's View of Hell." The cartoon depicts a tuxedo-clad conductor lifting his baton in musical leadership. The entire orchestra in front of him consists of banjo players.

The banjo gets a bad rap in that the instrument (of African origins) is associated with unfortunate stereotypes. Folks of my age can remember vividly "The Ballad of Jed Clampett" and its performers, Flatt & Scruggs, appearing on the 1960's sitcom *The Beverly Hillbillies*. Then there's *Deliverance*.

Bluegrass music appeals to me. I suppose primarily it is the virtuosi musical talents represented by bluegrass instruments. Each soloist steps up to a microphone and unleashes a blazing acoustical solo.

Banjo, Guitar, Fiddle (never violin!), and Mandolin were the stars of the show for this young musician.

At University of Georgia I sang in the University of Georgia Men's Glee Club, and as an added treat played in the UGAMG-CBAOFRG. What's that you ask?

The University of Georgia Men's Glee Club (By Audition Only) Folk Rock Group was a fine group of players and singers.

I met a banjo virtuoso there from Lincolnton, Georgia. His name was Jim Atkins and he did a hilarious imitation of Donald Duck in addition to playing the daylights out of a Gibson Mastertone Banjo. Jim acquired a life-long nickname: "Duck Adkins." He has delighted audiences for decades with his humor and banjo playing. He is still at it today, and we are better for it.

We put together a bluegrass/Americana band back in those college days called "Farrell Pitts and His All-Star Band." Farrell played a vintage Gibson and served as the lead singer. I played lead acoustic guitar and John Harriman (a cello virtuoso) played bass. My college roommate, Bruce Sellers (who would become an internationally lauded tenor) sang and played washboard. Two delightful sopranos, Kathy Bridges Melton and Andie Reed sang back up.

We opened our brief career with a concert at The Baptist Center at The University of Georgia. The modern chapel was a terrific setting acoustically and we often sang there after weekday lunches.

The side door opened and we walked into the performing space single file. The audience erupted into a combination of applause and yells that, frankly, I don't know if I have ever experienced since. Bass player Harriman turned to me with shock on his face and he mouthed a word not suitable for a family newspaper.

American music lost a real treasure just a few weeks ago. Guitar genius Tony Rice, already in poor health, was taken from us suddenly and completely. The guitar social media lit up with tributes, videos, and words of adoration.

My dear friend and beloved musical brother Dan Crary (equally beloved in bluegrass circles) communicated with me almost immediately. Dan and Tony have shared stages all over the world. The two basically created a space for the solo acoustic guitar in a bluegrass milieu that heretofore was dominated by banjo, fiddle, and mandolin.

Dan and I met during an edition of The Rome International Film Festival, and it was at this fateful breakfast at a downtown eatery that he told me how much he loved my children's book "Martin the Guitar." It was Dan's kind recommendation to a publisher that started "Martin" on its delightful journey.

I visited Dan one fall weekend at a big guitar festival in rural Tennessee. We played in the hotel room together and then Dan suggested we go down to the lobby and pick with some of the participants.

When Dan entered the room, the place fell quiet. The awe on the faces of the assembled pickers was extraordinary. Dan introduced me, and we played some traditional bluegrass tunes with the guitarists, and all the while Dan regaled the folks with stories, tips, and existential philosophy. You see, bluegrass guitarist Dan Crary is not only an American treasure; he also possesses an earned PhD.

Rome's excellent bluegrass players no doubt mourned the passing of Tony Rice. A number of them shared their grief and admiration on social media. There are great players like the excellent Roger Dees in Rome and they can often be heard at local bluegrass festivals. Before I moved to New Mexico, I often played Bluegrass Gospel Music with Rome composer Stan Pethel and his talented sons. It was always a treat.

More recently I toured the United Kingdom and played at a little hall they call Carnegie in New York City. I was lucky in that my friend, conductor, composer, and banjo player Tim Sharp, recently retired Executive Director of the American Choral Directors Association, invited me to play guitar on his delightful bluegrass mass "Come Away to the Skies: A High Lonesome Bluegrass Mass."

European audiences embraced the sound of the banjo and friends as we played in concert halls, churches, and even the Guinness Brewery in Dublin, Ireland.

The Irish bluegrass musicians we played with knew more about bluegrass music than we did. They remain friends to this day.

Dial the bluegrass channel on your Pandora or similar streaming device. I guarantee your foot will tap and your head will nod in time to the music. Also, check out the late Tony Rice and the eternal Dan Crary.

As the bumper sticker proclaims, "My Grass is Blue."

January 2021

Music and Place

In 1973 an unknown singer from the suburbs of Birmingham, Alabama, recorded his first LP in a basement studio known as Sound of Birmingham. The resulting album produced a minor hit, "I've Been Lonely for so Long" which led to the work being distributed by the legendary Memphis label Stax. His name was Frederick Knight.

Why do I know this?

For Christmas this year, my brilliant son enrolled me in a vinyl record program produced by a company known as VMP Classics. Every so often a beautiful LP arrives at my New Mexico door, and each delivery has contained a treat.

This month it was Frederick Knight's album and last month it was a soundtrack, also recorded for Stax, by the legendary Isaac Hayes, who most of my readers know from either the soundtrack to *Shaft* or as the character Chef on the animated television series *South Park*.

Both recordings are similar in style and substance. The albums feature huge production teams sporting large horn sections, backup singers, and lots of funky percussion. The music makes for excellent dinner preparation soundtracks and, most certainly, house dancing.

Coincidentally, I watched a brilliant documentary for the second time last week entitled *Muscle Shoals*. This film told the story of Fame Studios and its house band called The Swampers. Aretha, Wilson Picket, Paul Simon, and even the Rolling Stones encamped to northern Alabama and produced some of their most renowned recordings.

When asked about the "magic" of Muscle Shoals, several musicians pointed out the nearby Tennessee River. The recording studios of Memphis have The Big Muddy less than a few blocks away, and indeed Frederick Knight had The Cahaba River at his doorstep.

Music and space are important. That gumbo of The South and its rhythm and blues music has long been recognized as a real thing.

Sorry, Montana friends, but those long prairie stretches may inspire some great poetry, but no major American musical forms have emerged from those fields of waving grain.

American icon Bo Diddley lived here in Valencia County, New Mexico, for a brief time, but his music is never described as that "New Mexico Beat."

What made LA's Laurel Canyon a mecca for music of the early 1960's? Something about those rolling hills, cheap rents, and permissive atmosphere drew Frank Zappa, Joni Mitchell, and even The Monkees to create memorable melodies and rhythm.

The same environment drew young musicians to Athens, Georgia, and that milieu gave birth to REM, The B52's, Pylon, and more, yet both Laurel Canyon and Athens, Georgia are no longer the cradles of music culture that thrived for a time.

I think that when these examples of "lightening in a bottle" occur, the protagonists are generally unaware of an emergence of a "newness."

Two folks get together and find a mutual affection for music past. Susan writes poetry and Lauren plays the piano. Johnny likes to play his guitar loud. A pizza joint owner sees cheap, but talented young musicians as a way to boost his Friday night deep-dish sales.

It happened in the early sixties in Austin, Texas. A run-down storefront, actually just a shell of a space, became a music venue for local Texas musicians and eventually lured blues greats like Muddy Waters and Lightning Hopkins. Seeds for cultural blossomings were planted.

Oh, did I mention? The local folks, as in the grownups, hated it. Somehow the music thrived and inspired.

So where's it happening today?

Nashville has moved from its country conservative platform to a wide variety of musical forms. Songwriting is still king in

Music City, but one doesn't have to look very far to find musical explorers of a most diverse kind. Brooklyn? New Orleans?

Actually, right now, it's a bedroom.

Musicians of all stripes have retreated to their bedrooms during this time of Quarantine. Armed with a laptop, a microphone, some music software, and tons of imagination, folks from Portland to Jacksonville are producing the music of our time.

My studio here at Ranchero Musselwhite would normally be a bedroom, but instead provides a space where I record all sorts of music using real and electronic instruments. The bathroom for this room is a Voice Over recording space rendered acoustically dead by all sorts of sound absorbing materials.

Just as the internet de-centralized society, music making has become an intimate act which, in a matter of seconds, can be recorded and shared with the entire world. Now instead of CBGB's it's 22 Oak Street, Anywhere, USA.

Here's to the next generation.

February 2021

Seret and Sons

At the corner of Galisteo and West Alameda in old Santa Fe sits the emporium of Seret and Sons. In 1980 during my stint at The Santa Fe Opera I would often walk up Galisteo to the now shuttered Galisteo News in order to grab a coffee and read the newspaper. I would glance across the street and marvel at exotic storefront of Seret and Sons.

I've never been to Morocco or Algeria, but upon entering the huge antique doors of the shop one is immediately transported to a magical and fictitious land of Ali Baba and the mythical forty thieves.

The first large room is filled to all corners with every matter of rugs and floor coverings. A myriad of colors assaults the senses as if one was afloat in an inky ocean. There are huge rugs, runners, wall hangings, and more that seem to have been transported from some ancient potentate's palace aboard creaky sailing ships.

One room gives way to others like a labyrinth. I've stepped into Seret and Sons for over forty years and never fully explored its riches.

Usually one is greeted by a salesperson who always maintains a certain quietude. The business is notable for its calmness. There is no artificial music piped in to create an artificial atmosphere. The emporium is filled with magical ambience.

Actress Carol Burnett said about Santa Fe, "Santa Fe is the only place in the world where you pick out your front door before you decide on the rest of the house." Seret and Sons is filled with ornate doors, doorframes, and architectural elements.

Carved portals adorned with fanciful elephants lean against adobe walls. Wrought iron crescents resting against a pillar wait for just the right home.

My favorite area at Seret and Sons is actually outside the store in back. There is a large lot at the rear where one's imagination is snared by ornate gates, doorways, and window frames. They are stacked, or I should say, leaned, in groups of ten and twenty. The pathways between the museum pieces barely accommodate a person.

A short while ago my wife and I paid a visit to the yard of antiquities. We recently had a coyote fence constructed at the edge of our portale or patio. Our fence ends with a short sidewalk linking the area with our carport. We designed the fence with Seret and Sons in mind. In short, we hoped to find the perfect door.

There is a mind-boggling array of treasures in the Seret and Sons back lot and we had measurements, a tape measure, and an open mind as our guide listened thoughtfully to our needs. Miraculously, we spotted a Moroccan door festooned with ancient ironwork, and more so, the doorway matched the dimensions of the fence opening with perfection.

The artisans who installed our coyote fence affixed the doorway with ease, and the project took on a finished aura.

After all those years of looking in the windows and peering into the back area of Seret and Sons, we finally made a purchase.

I went back to Santa Fe this week seeking a companion purchase. I had in mind matching windows suspended from an iron frame that stands beside our outdoor fireplace. This time I had not only measurements, but also photographs of the now completed coyote fence and doorway.

What has Middle Eastern architectural elements and southwestern style have to do with each other?

For centuries the Santa Fe area has been a crossroads of culture, faith, and creativity. The cultures of Spain, native America, and Anglo (as in back east) commingle and provide a cultural soup that continues to simmer today. I suppose that would explain the longevity of Seret and Sons.

The assistant at Seret and Sons led me through the winding hallways of the store out into the back yard. Within moments he found a pair of ancient window shutters that were the brother and sister to our Moroccan door, and indeed the pair now hangs gracefully at the edge of our portale.

New Mexico is called the Land of Enchantment, and one of those enchanting elements surely is the free flowing commerce between art and architecture. Others jokingly call this area the Land of Entrapment. I think there may be a bit of truth in both.

May 2021

New Mexico's Enchanted Spell

We are still in Monsoon season in New Mexico, and this year has been a watery blessing. If you follow the national weather scene you know that the American southwest has been dry, dry, dry. Most of us do not have lawns to water out here in New Mexico, but the big alfalfa fields in my neck of the woods have really suffered.

With a low snowpack up in the Sangre de Christo Mountains and beyond, my nearby Rio Grande River often slows to a trickle. The river provides the water for our Rio Abajo crops and things have been grim.

The last few weeks, however, have brought heavy winds and accompanying thunderstorms. Even my skin feels replenished and the cool morning temperatures allow me to sit out here on my portale and write a column.

I've become very "New Mexicanized" in my time out here. I am sitting on a portale (porch) looking at my coyote fence (doesn't really keep coyotes out) and drinking New Mexico pinion coffee (coffee brewed with pinion nuts.)

Yesterday the bride and I celebrated our thirty year wedding anniversary by going to an Albuquerque restaurant called Farm and Table. The eatery features food grown by New Mexico artisanal farmers and the setting is southwestern strong with adobe walls, wrought iron furniture and our delicious home grown Gruet Champagne.

Just south of me is the object of much recent attention. Richard Branson's Spaceport sits out in the desert, and the world came to see his spacecraft leap into space. Observing this, writer Molly Jong-Fast declared, "New Mexico is the best state!" Since I am presently writing for a Georgia newspaper, I gently pause an affirmation to this statement, but she wrote what she wrote.

At the spaceport, our terrific governor, Michele Lujan Grisham, was there looking sharp in her tres chic cowboy boots and southwestern jewelry. She was all smiles standing next to billionaire Branson.

Ms. Lujan Grisham took the Covid challenge head on, and as a result New Mexico is one of the leading states in the nation in terms of per-capita vaccination success. This is quite an accomplishment given the size of the state and its scattered population.

The nearby Navajo Nation, at first devastated by Covid deaths, has completely risen to the challenge, and they are justifiably proud of their successful vaccination campaign. The wife and I recently traveled through the Navajo Nation, and road signs touted the importance of vaccination and vax clinics dotted the enormous region. The Navajo or Dine are independent minded Native Americans. Good on them.

From Native American pottery to the brand spanking new NBC/Universal Studio complex, the arts hold a place of honor in this state. The great artisans have now returned to the portale on the Santa Fe Square (thanks again, Governor Lujan-Grisham!) and downtown Albuquerque is festooned with those ubiquitous bright yellow placards directing actors and crew to film locations. The fantastic Balloon Fiesta is now on the calendar and we all look forward to seeing the morning sky filled with hundreds of hot air balloons.

National treasure and renowned artist Judy Chicago ("The Dinner Party") lives about five miles from my house and she continues to create her art from her home in a restored Belen, New Mexico, hotel. She and the forward-thinking mayor of Belen, the young and vibrant Jerah R. Cordova, have conspired and created an arts district right in the middle of this historic New Mexico town.

It's not perfect out here in the Land of Enchantment. There's poverty, drug and gang issues (just like Georgia!), and a real challenge in feeding and educating children due to the vagaries of society in the 21st Century.

New Mexico is blessed with forward thinking and engaged leadership from the state house (which we call "The Roundhouse") to the tiny city hall in Belen, New Mexico. Political grandstanding is at a minimum (except during election season, meh!). Another political point of pride is that a member of nearby Laguna Pueblo, Deb Haaland, was appointed by President Biden to be the first Native American Secretary of the Department of the Interior. How cool is that? From support of the arts, public health, our fragile planet, and concern for fellow human beings, New Mexico is a shining beacon.

I wish it for all.

July 2021

Neighbors

Do you have neighbors? Do you have neighborly neighbors?

My writing partner, the great Donald J. Davenport, lives in a lovely neighborhood north of Santa Fe, New Mexico. He has never spoken of his neighbors, but I do know that he despises a certain giant plastic flamingo that dominates the street to his house. The flamingo is one of those 'arty' mailbox facades, and that's all the print I am going to dignify this heinous plastic bird.

Growing up on Hillcrest Drive in Thomson, Georgia, was a blast. One of the reasons I have such fond memories is that in the summer the adults would gather with lawn chairs (you know, the kind with plastic webbing that would always pinch your legs?) in a backyard and grill, sip drinks, and tell tall tales.

While the adults adulted, the kids would play chase, freeze tag, and share our own versions of tall tales.

The neighbors were there with a ladder if needed or a ride to a school activity. Because we were southern, the kids addressed the adults with a "Miss Jane" or a "Mr. Charles." It was a sign of respect and we thought nothing about it.

I had several outstanding neighbors in Rome during my thirty years in place. Neighbors who would visit the hospital if appropriate or others would gather the mail while we were on vacation.

Out here, I have three neighbors, all who have become a wonderful part of our lives. We are neighbors by geography in that the lane we share is a dead end and so we have no traffic to bother with, mostly.

My neighbor to the east, Barb, is a recently retired professional, and we meet several times a week at our mailbox line and catch up on the area news. Barb, like us, is a dog lover, and our pups usually run to greet her and gently rear up and say hello. Her pups are larger than ours and provide security from anyone who may wander down into her yard from the acequia, or ditch.

Barb feeds the local feral cats, and one or two skunks that mosey into her yard. The stinkers hunker down at the cat bowl and share an evening meal.

Just across the lane from Ranchero Musselwhite is Mr. Bob, whose name adorns our road. Bob is retired and was a very successful contractor. He is generous to a fault, in that he offers his tractor skills (which are considerable), and he lends me a ladder when I have to do some aerial work on my side of the road.

Bob has two dogs, Sally and Jackson, and they live right across from our mailboxes. I take treats to the two dogs most every day when I go out to check the mail. I take Bob his mail and newspaper and place it quietly on his backyard table.

Neighbors, don't you know.

I hate to throw out magazines, so I make a stack of my New Yorker Magazines and deliver them to Bob. I take others and share with Barb. All that great writing needs to be shared.

I save for last my neighbor Ramon. As my late mother would say, "He is a pistol." By that I mean he is a way cool person with theories, opinions, and ideas that never run dry. He is retired from the US Postal Service and is a nicely educated intellectual, but he would run from that term in a New Mexico minute.

His apple trees this season are so full that they are bowed with the weight of the fruit. I was pulling out of the neighborhood last week and he flagged me down.

He said, "You have got to take some of these apples!"

I replied in the affirmative thinking that he would take a plastic shopping bag and deliver a couple of dozen. When I returned to the house later that morning, my wife indicated a plastic crate brimming with fresh fruit. My oh my.

Ramon and I have a common dilemma. New Mexico ground squirrels are getting into the engine compartments of our trucks and being very, very naughty. Ramon and I share various remedies from putting fragrant soap bars in the engine compartment to, well, less peaceful responses.

Shared neighbor challenges.

My wife and I recently did one of our national tours in order to celebrate in person the first birthday of our grandson in Auburn, Alabama, where his parents work in education. I dutifully reported our absence to the neighbors, who promised to keep an eye out for strangers, or strange things.

I parked my truck at Bob's across the lane to remove it from squirrel mischief, and upon my return, I walked across the street to fetch my truck. Bob was in possession of a spare key, and seeing me approach, he met me in the middle of the lane. He said his phone had just rung and he answered to Ramon's familiar voice.

His message may just be the most neighborly thing I've heard of in quite a while. What did he tell Mr. Bob?

Two words.

"They're back."

August 2021

New Mexico Market Time

I have written in these pages before of the agrarian nature of the Rio Grande Valley where I live. Alfalfa fields are in full bloom all around Ranchero Musselwhite, and the two lane roads are busy with huge reapers and bailing machines.

Green Chile season is here in full tilt, and yesterday I peeled roasted chiles purchased fresh from the nearby Sichler Market. The market opened just under two weeks ago and I previously drove by the entrance hoping that they would open early this year. But true to form, the farm company's opening was right on schedule.

Our market is one of two. The other market is located a couple of hours south of Los Lunas in tiny San Antonio, New Mexico. San Antonio is famous for a pair of burger restaurants that produce one of the state's treasures: the green chile cheeseburger. The food networks have visited both cafes even though it is located in such a rural place.

I am lucky in that our Sichler Market sits around one mile from the gates to my home. Giant chile roasters dominate the outside area, and this time of the year local folks line up to purchase baskets of raw green chile. They then take them outside and hand them over to a very busy roasting crew.

The smell is incredible, and once smelled, it stays with your olfactory memory the entire year.

This past Saturday I drove to the market to pick up some tomatoes, but there were so many folks waiting for their roasted green chiles, I simply toured the parking lot and exited.

The market is one large room surrounded by doors and windows that stay open all day long. On the south side large crates dominate an area dedicated to fresh tomatoes.

Too many southern newspaper columnists grab the low hanging fruit (see what I did there?) and write about the glories of tomatoes and ensuing sandwiches.

I will only go to say that I have had no luck growing tomatoes here on the Ranchero, but the Sichler Market provides and boy howdy! The fruit are large, succulent and have none of the plastic taste of supermarket tomatoes. I know that locals buy the tomatoes in bulk in order to can homemade salsa, and one day I'm going to do this. Heck, the ingredients are right there, shoulder to shoulder, at the Sichler Market.

Two distinct areas dominate the north side of the market. One features large and small baskets of chiles. Some are pre-roasted and bagged. They are labeled according to the heat level within.

An adjacent aisle features various vegetables such as onions, potatoes, several kinds of squash, and another New Mexico favorite, huge bags of dried pinto beans. At the Sichler Market one can purchase beans by the tons, it seems. I buy modest amounts and keep them at hand for a delicious protein meal flavored with, you guessed it, green chile.

Near a melon area Sichler employees were stringing ristras the other day. We have a number of decorative red ristras around our home, including two giant ones that guard our front door. As you might guess, red chiles are simply ripened green chiles. Ristras are red chiles strung together and are primarily decorative. They also make a lovely Christmas wreath.

Did you know you can buy New Mexico red chiles at local Rome, Georgia, grocery stores? They sit in bags right on the end cap, or at least they were there a number of years ago in what they call the "Mexican" section.

I make red chile sauce from scratch. I use red chiles softened in boiling water, onions, broth, garlic, and cumin, coriander, and salt combined in a blender to create a tasty gravy. I used to strain the concoction, but now I just really hit "puree" and make a thicker sauce. Some great native New Mexican women who know their chile lore recommended the rougher method, and I now I favor it. I put the sauce on everything from eggs to pork, and usually find a good tortilla from Albuquerque's Frontier Restaurant to accompany.

Sichler's Market is old school, in that when one enters, greeting calls come from whoever is working the register or stocking beans. A splendid language soup of English and Spanish lofts over the room and gives this simple market a true Land of Enchantment atmosphere.

Incidentally, we live on old Sichler property. They were a German family who emigrated to the southwest and set up a farming empire. In my neighbor Barb's backyard is a tiny old west style cemetery that guards the remains of these olden inhabitants. I would like to think they approve of my affection for the market that bears their name.

Let's head to the market and see what's for dinner.

September 2021

Coffee

J.S. Bach liked coffee so much that he composed a cantata extolling its virtues. I love the fact that his "Coffee Cantata," as it is known, was first performed in a coffee house.

I like coffee and I love the smell of brewing coffee. Something about the rich aroma excites my brain cells. Perhaps it's the remembrance of entering a café or kitchen from winter's cold and being simultaneously greeted by that familiar blast of warm air and the smell of brewing java.

The old school diners in New York City sport huge coffee machines that dominate the counter behind short order cooks. These chrome vessels release that golden liquid with a steamy accompaniment, and let's face it, that classic New York white coffee cup is iconic in shape and function.

Starbucks. There, I said it. Speaking of New York City, I can remember a time when it was one of the city's points of pride that there were no Starbucks to be found. Now, it seems, there's a Starbucks on every corner.

I miss the coffee at northwest Georgia's Dirt Town Deli. When I was a part of the crew (and how I miss them!), we all had our own coffee mug, and when we arrived on our appointed day, our mugs would be lined up on the counter waiting our retrieval.

Upon arrival at the Dirt Town Deli, we would greet the owners and go directly to the coffee cup counter, fix the brew to our own personal tastes, and sit down at a round table before taking that first delicious sip. Sublime.

Swift & Finch Coffee arrived on Rome's Broad Street, and I don't think they've ever had a down day. The coffee house has regulars ranging from fundamentalist Christians to liberal college professors. I used to love talking film and book creation with Rome's Monica Shepard at Swift & Finch. A rotating cast of characters would stop and speak to Monica and she greeted them all with a personal story.

My beloved friend Kathryn Nobles is a regular at Swift & Finch, and she has become a coffee aficionado. She and her family frequently travel to America's national parks, and I can only imagine the smell of fine coffee wafting around those campfires framed by majestic peaks.

My first teaching job was at Sam Houston State University in Huntsville, Texas. The music school had a coffee club located just down the hall from my voice studio, and in between lessons I would walk down the hall, fix a cup, and join in what conversation that transpired.

I found out pretty quickly that my body couldn't handle massive quantities of the caffeinated brew. Mid-afternoon I started to wonder if I had some sort of neurological issue, and it occurred to me there might be an issue with too much coffee. I cut down and then had more conversation than coffee. My body responded in a healthy way.

Once in a while I will fix a cup and walk across the dirt lane outside Ranchero Musselwhite and catch up on the news with my neighbors Bob and Ramon. We sit outside on Bob's porch and ponder nearby construction, the local elections, or the state of college football.

One delightful coffee related discovery I have made out here in New Mexico is the existence of New Mexico Piñon Coffee. Made with roasted piñon pine nuts, this coffee creates a rich brew, and oh the smell!

The company started twenty-five years ago in the bed of a 1952 Chevy pickup truck, and the coffee is now a New Mexico state treasure. The gentleman who started the company even had a pet dog named, wait for it, Decaf.

On an overnight visit to Santa Fe recently, the coffee in the hotel lobby was 100% New Mexico Piñon Coffee. They even sold it next to the check-in counter.

I brew my morning pot with ⅓ New Mexican piñon and ⅔ decaf. The piñon flavor boosts the decaf, and the combination suits me just fine.

No matter how you take it, black, with cream, or as espresso, I lift my cup to you this sunny New Mexico morning. Tell the folks at Dirt Town Deli or Swift & Finch I said hello!

November 2021

Christmas in New Mexico

The Cibola Forest sits on the shoulders of the Manzano Mountains. Much of the forest is uninhabited, and it is there that my family has established a brand new tradition: the cutting of a Christmas tree.

My bride and I live in a very modern home that has for the good, very high ceilings, and for the lesser, very high ceilings. A normal sized Christmas tree looks, well, puny in our surroundings.

For the first few years of living in our New Mexico home, we would travel to Santa Fe and purchase a tall tree that would suit our home. Along with the tall height of the tree came a similar tall price tag.

Last year our son, due to pandemic scheduling, came out here early and easily did his work on his laptop. He accompanied us into the depths of the Cibola Forest and we found a lovely, yet imperfect forest specimen.

Oh, one has to purchase a tree-cutting permit from the state office. The cost? A whopping ten American dollars. Such a bargain.

This year the bride and I set out without number one son. We found the familiar forest service road just off the main drag leading into Mountainair, New Mexico. We set the odometer and we went, as we say, off the grid.

I called my great neighbor, Mr. Silver, just before we departed from Ranchero Musselwhite and alerted him to our quest. I told him if he didn't see the returning truck before sunset to call the cavalry.

It was a rambunctious drive on Forest Service Road 422. We traveled almost nine miles before the terrain out our window changed from grasslands dotted with pinion to more mountainous fare. We were alone.

The road resembled a large cheese grater in that rocks and small boulders dominated large patches of the dirt road. Our average speed was around five miles per hour.

Along the way we spotted desolate ranches that were so forlorn they appeared to be abandonded. We slowed to navigate washed out creases on the primitive thoroughfare, and roared to an astounding ten miles per hour on certain brief smoother stretches.

Eventually we began a slight ascent, and the terrain changed. Evergreens dominated the sides of the road, and sharp arroyos beckoned down below. We observed what we called "baby Christmas trees."

Around mile ten I spotted a potential candidate, but we felt its symmetry was lacking. I slowed the truck down and rolled down the windows. The air was filled with a fresh pinion fragrance, and the cool mountain breeze was invigorating.

To our right, a spruce tree stood by the side of the road waving seductively.

I stopped the truck and the bride hopped out for an initial assessment.

"This one might work," she called.

I pulled the truck over and got out. The silence was deafening. Nobody behind us, nobody in front, and the wind whistling through the forest was a balm for the soul.

I stepped down the steep side of the road, and knew immediately that this tree was the one. I reached into the back of the truck for our battery powered chainsaw, and between quick work from the two of us, we had our new Christmas tree in the back of the pickup.

A lovely sense of joy came over us as I turned the truck back down the mountain. Even the road felt smoother. We glanced back to make sure the tree was secured, and out front we were rewarded with one of the great New Mexico vistas.

A couple of miles down the road we were greeted by two vehicles, one pulling a small open trailer. As we slowly passed, the driver rolled down her window and greeted us with a friendly smile.

"We've purchased our permit for a Christmas tree and are wondering how much farther up this road we might find a tree," she said.

I told her she was about two miles away and that there were a number of fine candidates on the east side of the forest road. She thanked me with a smile.

As she rolled up the window a voice rang out from the back seat of her vehicle.

"Merry Christmas," he said.

My wife and I immediately replied, "Merry Christmas."

Whether you buy your tree from a big box retailer, an independent lot, or venture into the great outdoors, we wish you a very Merry Christmas from the Land of Enchantment.

December 2021

Season of Fire

We've received a number of messages over the last few weeks asking about our current safety. As I write this, wildfires rage all over the state, and if flames aren't enough, the current state of the air we breathe is problematical.

A couple of weeks ago, Easter weekend to be precise, I was driving back from a service in north Albuquerque that used me as a singer and beheld a huge column of smoke to the south. I immediately thought that a jet had crashed at the Sunport, but as I passed it, the huge plume was further south. I worried first about Isleta Pueblo with its heavily forested acreage, and then I worried more about my own home.

The fire was located on both sides of the Rio Grande in a woodland strip we call The Bosque. The fire raged about two miles or so from our house and even closer to the campus of University of New Mexico-Valencia where my wife is Dean.

Expert Navajo firefighters and tactical air support was summoned. It took a couple of days to defeat the fire and the devastation was horrible to look upon.

At the same time, the town of Ruidoso several hours south of me was under attack and had to be evacuated. Many homes were lost and the mountain range down there was burned low.

Now several weeks out, there are several big fires throughout the state. One of my favorite New Mexico cities, Las Vegas, is threatened.

As I look out my front windows, the Manzano Mountains are sitting in a great smoky haze from north to south. Folks with any respiratory issues are urged to stay inside by the authorities.

Yesterday I had a coffee appointment with a young filmmaker in Albuquerque. I returned south mid-morning, and took my usual two-lane road through Isleta Pueblo toward my home.

There is a high point in Isleta, a bridge over the railway, where one can have an unobstructed view from the middle of the pueblo all the way to the Manzano Mountains. I always look over there and admire the dramatic mountain vista.

Something was different, however.

I'm guessing around fifteen to twenty miles away, there appeared to be a column of smoke at the base of the mountains. I slowed. Was it fire or a farmer working dust up in an alfalfa field? Wisps of grey smoke appeared to swirl and then head north in the prevailing winds.

It's pretty desolate over there. Perhaps a few homesteads, maybe a handful of reclusive Native Americans, or empty Forest Service land.

I was quickly off the bridge and down in the river valley where I live. I pondered and pondered. Should I call? Who should I call? They are already so busy. Would I sound like a crackpot?

When I arrived at home minutes later, I went to the computer and found the number for the closest ranger station.

Connie answered the phone, and she was completely professional. She asked questions about what did I see, what color(s) the smoke/dust were, did it appear to be moving, and more. She took some personal information from me, and when I semi-apologized for bothering them, she expressed appreciation for caring enough to call. She asked if I would mind if someone else called me.

Ten minutes later a Forest Ranger called and asked even more pointed questions about what I saw and where I saw it. He too was calm, professional, and extremely thorough. Fire fighting is serious business in New Mexico.

He informed me that he had a fire lookout stationed at the top of the Manzano Mountains and he would contact her by radio and see if she could spot anything.

Can you imagine? All alone, male or female, on top of a desolate mountain, well ,desolate if you count the bears and rattlesnakes, and only armed with a walking stick and a pair of binoculars.

The ranger also indicated that there were colleagues in the valley below who were firewatchers, and he would reach out to them.

He thanked me for calling and told me that it was no problem at all for citizens to report issues as they find them.

I don't know how this unfolded. I hope it wasn't a fire, but agricultural in nature. The air is thick with particulate matter this morning, and this thickness is spread all over the state.

I feel pretty safe here at Ranchero Musselwhite. We do have our local fire department at hand, and there are plenty of roads in and out of our community should we have to evacuate.

Folks talk about preparing "go bags" of important stuff if one has to make a hasty departure.

It is not ironic to note that New Mexico was the home to the most famous fire-fighting icon of all, Smokey Bear. It's not Smokey the Bear, mind you, but enough of that.

Keep us in mind out here, and pray for those fire-whipping winds to die down and soon.

May 2022

Acknowledgements

I like to believe that I lived in the golden age of columnists who wrote for *The Atlanta Journal-Constitution*. I adored Lewis Grizzard despite that fact that he hated two of my favorite things: opera and broccoli. His affection for The University of Georgia was shared enthusiastically in my small town Georgia home.

I read Ron Hudspeth and imagined I would sit close to him in the Northside Tavern or Harrison's on Peachtree and hear the tall tales of Pete the Northside Barkeep. Sports columnist and writer Furman Bisher wrote sports poetry that told of mythical clashes between SEC football powers. I hung on his every word.

The queen of *AJC* columnists, Celestine Sibley, was a much-loved writer and I treasure a letter she wrote to me after one of my columns was published in her beloved newspaper.

These folks were my writing heroes, and I imagined that one day I would write a regular column in some imaginary newspaper. Thanks to the legendary opinion page editor Pierre-Rene Noth at *The Rome News-Tribune,* I got my chance.

Well into my writing time at the *RN-T,* I was invited to a breakfast club at a hole-in-the-wall joint about a half hour above Rome, Georgia. The place had the improbable name of The Dirt Town Deli. It was there I befriended two master newspaper writers, Lee Walburn and Norman Arey. Little did I know that these two were close friends with the aforementioned *AJC* writers, and that I would sit and listen to these two regale me with stories of folks whose veins ran with newspaper ink.

Soon I called Lee Walburn a mentor, and I still do today. I am deeply grateful for these inspirational human beings.

I thank the editor of this book, the erudite and class act that is Richard Jay Hutto. His writing on the Gilded Age, Royalty, and Georgia's Jekyll Island stands tall, and his keen eye brought my manuscript to his exacting standards. Mr. Hutto is not only my colleague, but also a family friend. Our friendship is still strong and continuing having begun as fellow undergraduates at The University of Georgia.

I stand in appreciation for the continued support of my editors at *The Rome News-Tribune,* John Bailey and Diane Wagner. They have generously offered their written support herein, and their encouragement on a monthly basis is appreciated beyond measure.

Highest gratitude must be given to Dekie Hicks of Wheredepony Press and her effervescent attitude upon taking on this book project. She is patient, kind, and a treasure to the writing community.

I give thanks to my screenwriting partner, Donald J. Davenport. His love for great writing matches mine, and our hours of writing, scheming, producing, and podcasting have enriched my life in New Mexico beyond description.

I offer sincere and enthusiastic thanks to the two professionals who represent me in the entertainment industry. Lynette O' Connor, of Albuquerque's O' Agency keeps my name and face before casting directors and producers with class, energy and aplomb. I am proud to call her my agent and to reside on her distinguished roster. Kathy Olsen, my manager at Encompass Arts, continues to champion my work throughout the world with unflagging enthusiasm. Our decades-long friendship grows and blossoms as her advice and leadership continues to joyously inform the work I do.

A big tip of my hat goes to the readers of my columns over the years who have responded with letters, notes, emails, and shouts of encouragement on the street. As the cliché goes, "It's nice to be read."

Finally I give thanks and acknowledgement to my family. My son Austin Musselwhite always responds to my expressions of nerves before a big project with "You've got this, Dad." My daughter Dory Musselwhite Thompson and her talented husband Eric Thompson are ardent cheerleaders. Their son, Henry, is the dedicatory subject of this book.

To my talented, smart, and ever patient wife, Laura, I cannot express enough appreciation for her continued support. I am a lucky fellow indeed. She has never called me back when I head for my writing room with an "I'm going to write." She has my heart.

www.ingramcontent.com/pod-product-compliance
Lightning Source LLC
Chambersburg PA
CBHW071449030726
47593CB00003B/963

9781735760469